ROLL AGAIN

Roll Again

A BOOK OF GAMES TO PLAY

collated and edited
by Jon Stone and Kirsten Irving

sidekickBOOKS

First published in 2022 by
SIDEKICK BOOKS
www.sidekickbooks.com

Printed by
ImprintDigital

Typeset in Libre Baskerville and Raleway

Copyright of text and images remains with the authors.

Kirsten Irving and Jon Stone have asserted their right to be identified as the editors of this work under Section 77 of the Copyright, Designs and Patents Act 1988.

Sidekick Books asserts that under Section 30A of the Copyright, Designs and Patents Act 1988 this work should be treated as pastiche, and that reasonable use of excerpts from copyrighted works therefore does not infringe copyright.

All rights reserved.

No part of this book may be reproduced, stored in a retrieval system or transmitted in any form without the written permission of Sidekick Books.

Cover design / typesetting by Jon Stone
ISBN: 978-1-909560-28-4

Overleaf: *Untitled game showing children with geese, and many animals, flowers, etc.* (1930), artist unknown

From the John Johnson Collection of Printed Ephemera at the Bodleian Library, Oxford.

> All reality is caught up in the play of the concepts which designate it.

— Jacques Ehrmann, Cathy Lewis and Phil Lewis, 'Homo Ludens Revisited', *Yale French Studies* No. 41: 'Game, Play, Literature' (1968)

> I'm on the side that's always lost against the side of Heaven. I'm on the side of snake-eyes tossed against the side of Seven.

— Leonard Cohen, 'The Captain' (1984)

CONTENTS

"If someone says ..."   *15*

SUSAN COOLIDGE
Word and Question   *19*
UNKNOWN
Death is a Fool   *21*
EDWIN EVANS-THIRLWELL
13 games to play with a black hole   *22*
SQUAMATE & RUNG
A Bunch of Lonesome Heroes   *26*
SEB MANLEY
Minibeasts   *28*
***
The Human Kite   *37*

"Sometimes there's pleasure ..."   *38*

CHARLES COTTON
Bone-Ace   *39*
WIT and REASON   *40*
H. G. WELLS
Little Wars   *42*
GILES GOODLAND
Psyche and Erosion   *44*

CAMILLE RALPHS
She Plays the Box Game   *48*
***
Stakeout   *50*

"Incomplete or ambiguous games …"   *52*

CLIFF HAMMETT
Tempo   *54*
CAPTAIN A. S. HARRISON
Knuckle Bones   *58*
ASTRA PAPACHRISTODOULOU
Shouty Full Moon   *62*
UNKNOWN
Hot Cockles   *64*
UNKNOWN
I apprenticed my son   *65*
KATE GREENAWAY
Shouting Proverbs   *66*
Queen Anne and Her Maids   *67*
Conundra / Medusa   *68*

"In the design of simulation-style …"   *70*

ROB WALTON
Mittball   *71*

CONWENNA RAY
Spicebush Silkmoth — 72
***
The Scavenger God — 74
CHARLOTTE HEATHER
Chronic Illness: The Tabletop RPG — 76
***
Library on Fire — 78
Near Dogluck Weir — 80
Paper Date — 86
Let's see you talk your way out of this — 90
LENNI SANDERS / JAMES VARNEY
That's no ant! — 94
GERARD MCKEOWN
Say It Again — 96
JO BRANDON
Who's Luckiest? — 97
LINDA BLACK
DRAW! — 98
EILEEN RAMOS
Show and Tall Tale — 100
LCC / GEN ZENDAHL / JOE RAUDI
The Glass Bead Game — 102
MARY WHITE
A Book House for Paper Dolls — 104

TRADITIONAL
Hyakumonogatari Kaidankai   *106*

"In Japanese culture ..."   *107*

LENNI SANDERS / JAMES VARNEY
Kill ... kill ... kill!   *108*

Notes and Acknowledgments   *110*
Contributors   *112*

This book contains a threaded introduction. It begins here and resumes at points throughout.

IF someone says, "I like games," you could interpret it in one of several ways, depending on the context. They might mean that they are untrustworthy, mischievous or playful in the way they handle interpersonal relationships. They might be referring somewhat obliquely to physical sports like snooker or tennis, or to betting or slot machines. More likely, you might think, they mean videogames or party games – low-stakes contests played out in a domestic setting – or tabletop games played with boards and counters, cards and/or dice. But even when you can establish the kind of game being talked about, there are still a great many aspects to gameplay that a person might specifically enjoy, and this can make it difficult to get a fix on what, if anything, is the common denominator in how games appeal to us.

Someone may, for instance, derive pleasure primarily from testing themselves against others, from establishing their own strengths and deficiencies. They may be seeking a feeling of triumph that evades them in their everyday duties. They may enjoy demonstrating a particular skill, or provoking allies and opponents in particular ways. They may enjoy pretending to be someone else, or imagining a world quite different to the one in which we live. They may thrill at being asked to make certain dramatic or consequential choices, at exercising temporarary power. They may take satisfaction in mastering a system to the point where it no longer presents them with any kind of challenge, or they may enjoy cooperating with other players, being put into a position where camaraderie comes naturally.

In this book we hope to have included something for every reader who enjoys games, whichever of the above applies to them. But in mixing up different kinds of games and presenting them in a somewhat improvised order, we also hope to (gently) induce you to think about the different ways in which even simple games speak to varied needs and inclinations, reflect or resist certain kinds of custom and rite, and overlap (or mingle) with literary forms. Every game here is presented as a set of rules or instructions, or as a text which in some way alludes to a set of rules or instructions. Most of these can be carried out in the ways you might expect, but where they cannot, or where, upon reading them, you feel no desire to carry them out (if, in other words, it's just not your type of game), you can still envisage the procedure in your mind's eye. This might lead you to adapt the text in some other fashion, to find pertinent meaning within it, or to reflect on what is missing that would otherwise convince you to play.

Approaching a set of game rules or instructions primarily as a text for reading, rather than as a means of facilitating gameplay, generates an encounter similar to that we might have with poetry: a world is briefly conjured that relates in some way to our own, events are alluded to or played out, and by close of play, some sense of indeterminacy remains. Something has *not* happened. A door is left open. Partly for this reason, and partly because we find the relationship between poetry and games interesting in other ways, we have included here works which are more poem than game, as well as a small number of extracts from longer texts which you could approach as incomplete games, or as 'found' or accidental poems.

We invite you, therefore, to both read and play, and to think about what it means to choose between the two modes. We also invite you to carry these considerations forward into your future encounters with games and literary texts alike.

SUSAN COOLIDGE
Word and Question
from What Katy Did at School (1873)

All the poems having been read, Katy now proposed that they should play 'Word and Question'. She and Clover were accustomed to the game at home, but to some of the others it was quite new.

Each girl was furnished with a slip of paper and a pencil, and was told to write a word at the top of the paper, fold it over, and pass it to her next left-hand neighbor.

"Dear me! I don't know what to write," said Mary Silver.

"Oh, write any thing," said Clover. So Mary obediently wrote "Any thing," and folded it over.

"What next?" asked Alice Gibbons.

"Now a question," said Katy. "Write it under the word, and fold over again. No, Amy, not on the fold. Don't you see, if you do, the writing will be on the wrong side of the paper when we come to read?"

The questions were more troublesome than the words, and the girls sat frowning and biting their pencil-tops for some minutes before all were done. As the slips were handed in, Katy dropped them into the lid of her work-basket, and thoroughly mixed and stirred them up.

"Now," she said, passing it about, "each draw one, read, and write a rhyme in which the word is introduced and the question answered. It needn't be more than two lines, unless you like. Here, Rose, it's your turn first."

"Oh, what a hard game!" cried some of the girls; but pretty soon they grew interested, and began to work over their verses.

"I should uncommonly like to know who wrote this abominable word," said Rose, in a tone of despair. "Clover, you rascal, I believe it was you."

UNKNOWN
Death is a Fool

"Je m'en vais enfin de ce monde, où il faut que le coeur se brise ou se bronze."
[And so I leave this world, where the heart must either break or turn to lead.]
—Nicolas Chamfort, 1794

For this game, you will need:
- an ordinary deck of cards
- a ring or hat into which to toss them

You're a French aphorist of the late 18th century, about to be arrested for publishing criticism of Robespierre, and of the Jacobin cause which you've all but abandoned. Your execution is likely; officers are on their way to your front door right now, and you've resolved not to be taken alive. You sit at your desk to write your last declaration.

Take the deck of cards and throw them one by one into the ring. For every one that lands face down, you've added one carefully weighed word to the paper. Each card that lands face-up is a hastier, more roughly cut word, but one that must suffice – there's too little time. Each card that misses the ring entirely must be retrieved and thrown again. When all 52 cards have landed in the ring, you are done. You've only to wait now for the beating of boots on the stairs.

EDWIN EVANS-THIRLWELL
13 games to play with a black hole

Having turned to this page you are suddenly in receipt of a cold and witty black hole of Martian-to-Saturnalian mass. The hole cannot be filled or denied, but here are some games you can play with it.

I. Begin by duplicating the hole for easier consumption: write any much larger text into the space described above until absolute opacity is achieved. You may experiment with other means of compression: for example, digestion, combustion or forgetfulness.

II. Place the hole unobtrusively on the floor during a party or work function. Any person who steps on the hole must assume the identity of the next person they see. Continue until there is only one person present.

III. Place the hole somewhere in a well-loved building. Tilt belongings in every room toward it. Anyone who finds the hole is obliterated and wins the game.

IV. Alternatively, have all but one player moan, laugh, sing or hiss at a volume proportionate to their distance from the hole. The remaining player must divine the hole's location by keeping quiet and listening carefully. (Upon finding tthe hole, the remaining player is instantly obliterated.)

V. Place the hole over a series of texts. Any occluded material never was, nor is that which remains a remainder. Prove this to one another by reading your text out, while attempting to discern what was never part of each other player's text. You can make use of gravitational lensing if you choose.

VI. Paste the hole over a clockface or display. For every moment that passes, players must agree on whether a moment has passed, and write or draw in the current time using white crayon or felt tip.

VII. Flip the paper over to redesignate the black hole as a white hole – a contemptible 'Get out of Jail Free' card that may be placed over any given *memento mori* in a public artwork, to universal derision. The author accepts no responsibility for any damage or embarrassment incurred during the whitewashing of black holes.

VIII. Recast the hole as a typographical dot – for example, a full stop, a bullet point or the dot on the letter *i* – in any given book, making your choice based on the best available knowledge of black-hole symptoms. Challenge other players to find it. For each failed attempt, rip pages from the book in proportion to the number of players, except for the page containing the black hole.

IX. Using any means, redesign the hole as a coin. Attempt to sneak the hole into the cash register of your local grocery or supermarket while buying an apple.

X. Pass the black hole from hand to hand in a circle while making ordinary conversation. Every time somebody receives the black hole, the last word they've uttered is swallowed and no longer able to be spoken. The game ends when it is no longer possible to speak.

XI. Infiltrate the black hole into any other hole-based recreational pastime.

XII. Seat the black hole at the table during a banquet. After every morsel they swallow, diners must take a fork or spoonful of food from their neighbour's plate and feed it to the hole. Anybody may, at any point, redesignate the black hole as a white hole in order to claim all the food it has eaten, to universal derision.

XIII. Spend quality time alone with the hole. Decide what it tastes, smells and feels like. Dissuade others of this.

SQUAMATE & RUNG
A Bunch of Lonesome Heroes
(A game which ends when you do)

This is a slow, open-ended role-playing game for one – though it may be made more sociable through conversations with others who are playing out their own version of it.

It's based on classical Chinese novels – in particular *Outlaws of the Marsh*, sometimes called *The Water Margin* – in which protagonists come and go, gather and disperse. You will need one or more keys in your possession (your own – they cannot be borrowed), access to a larder of poems, and a place to keep notes.

Over our lifetimes, we acquire many keys and give up or hand on the ones we had previously held. In this game, each key you own represents one of a party of vagabonds, of which you too are a member. Their backgrounds, ambitions and personalities vary greatly, but all of you are bound to a life of wandering. You keep each other company through fire and earthquake, outrage and intrigue, episode and incident. On occasion a new member joins (that is, you acquire a new key) and sometimes one or more of your band must depart (that is, you relinquish a key).

You are the party's record-keeper and myth-maker. You must make a note of everyone's names, as well as giving a very short account of the circumstances in which each arrived or departed. For the names you should use tiny fragments of existing poems, since this story takes place in the next world over, where the naming convention is rather different.

By way of suggestion:

Devil With Soft Laughter; *Pain-but-Pity*; *White Cocoon of Singing*; *The Sigh that Heaves the Grasses*; *Serried Mist*; *Ruffled Black Blossom*.

As to the details of coming and going, use these to gradually build an impression of the world in which your adventures take place. Make brief notes which imply a tale to be told:

Devil With Soft Laughter
JOINED 24th April 2021: *On the run from her mountain tribe after killing her father-in-law.*
LEFT 10th August 2022: *Disappeared during a battle in heavy snow on the bridge.*

Pain-but-Pity
JOINED 4th October 2021: *Lost a bet to Devil With Soft Laughter; made to carry her kit as payment.*
LEFT 11th October 2021: *Fell in love with a village girl.*

SEB MANLEY
Minibeasts

An intermittent two-player battle game expected to last for more than five hundred hours. At the end of the game you will have created your own trading card, which you may keep.

The game is divided into two phases: the Preparations Phase, which will last a long time, and the Battle Phase, which will not last very long at all.

PREPARATIONS PHASE

Select one of the Minibeasts character cards from the following pages (they can be found scattered throughout the book). This is your fighter.

Find someone who will play the game with you. This is your opponent. Your opponent must not live with you, but they may live anywhere else in the world.

Ask your opponent to select one of the remaining character cards. This is your opponent's fighter. Each player should play the game in their own home, as follows.

Make a copy of your character card and affix it to your fridge door in any prominent position. Your fighter has now begun preparations for battle.

Wait until someone notices the character card on the fridge door and comments on it. Ask that person to decide your fighter's Power value. They should do this by looking into the Minibeast's eyes and then writing a number between 0 and 100 in the box. (Note: You may not deliberately draw someone's attention to your card, nor may you entreat them to enter a certain value in the box.)

Ask the second person who comments on the character card to decide your character's Magic value.

Continue playing in this way until all five boxes contain a number.

Ask the sixth person who comments on the character card to colour in the fighter, using felt-tip pens.

Colour in the background of the character card yourself, using pencil crayons.

If you complete these steps before your opponent, write 'PB' ('Prepared Beast') in the little square on your character card. Your fighter has now finished preparations and is ready for battle.

If your opponent completes these steps before you, write

'UB' ('Unprepared Beast') in the little square on your character card. You now have ten days in which to complete your card. At this point you may move the card to any location inside your house. If your card attracts insufficient comments and you are unable to complete it, enter the worst possible value in each empty box (the worst value is the one furthest from the Optimum Value stated in the 'Table of Optimum Values').

When both players have completed their cards, begin the Battle Phase.

BATTLE PHASE

Compare your fighter's Power value to that of your opponent's fighter. Award one point to the fighter with the Power value closest to the Optimum Value (see 'Table of Optimum Values'). Do the same for the other four values. Award one extra point to the Prepared Beast. Whoever scores the most points is the winner of the battle. In the event of a tie, award victory to the Prepared Beast.

If you win the battle, draw a trophy in the little circle on your character card and display the card proudly.

If you lose the battle, draw a sad face in the little circle and place it in a shameful drawer forever.

TABLE OF OPTIMUM VALUES

Power	Magic	Confidence	Depravity	Insults
75	30	50	10 or 90	100

BEASTS

256 256

CRAZY
CAT

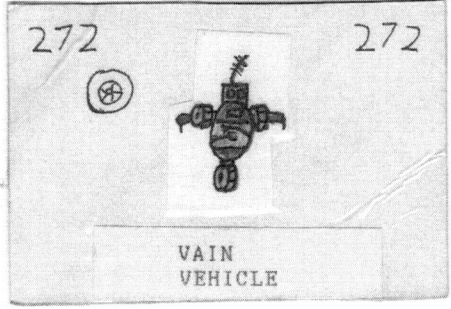

272 272

VAIN
VEHICLE

351 351

ANGRY
ANDROID

The Human Kite

You never meant to seize that stone
from the hidden drawer in the bedroom –
not for yourself, in any case. No –
you only wanted to determine its origin,
its rightful owner.
But it's yours now – it snuck into your palm,
between the bones of your hand, sits snug there,
making you light as a dandelion seed.

If only you knew how to use it.
If only you could stop yourself rising and unravelling
like thin smoke.

(THE GAME)
Thank goodness the stone also lets you tie yourself, invisibly, to other people. Once outdoors, you may only move through town by hooking onto a distant sleeve or collar and trailing behind its owner – until, that is, you need to change direction, at which time you must find a fresh anchor point.

You keep to well-populated areas.
You never grab a tow for too long.
You do your best impression
of something whose feet touch the ground.

Sometimes there's pleasure to be found in dedicating time to deciphering (and then intimately understanding) a set of oblique or complicated rules and procedures – particularly when dealing with archaic or specialist terminology, or any element of mathematical calculation. This too is surely a form of play, in the same way constructing a new game from scratch or adapting an existing game is regarded as inherently playful – or rather, simultaneously a creative, an industrious and a ludic act.

If a game in this book (or one you encounter elsewhere) cannot be properly understood, or if there are ambiguities in its rules, or the rules do not work in a way that serves the purposes of the player/s, rewriting, remaking, borrowing, improvising and combining are all legitimate avenues of exploration. Such responses also open up channels through which games and texts of differing natures become interwoven and continue to grow alongside one another.

CHARLES COTTON

Bone-Ace

from The Compleat Gamester (1674)

This game you may look on as trivial, and very inconsiderable, and so it is by reason of the little variety therein contained, but because I have seen ladies and persons of quality have played it for their diversion, I will briefly describe it, and the rather because it is a licking game for money.

There are seven, or eight (or as many as the cards will permit) play it at one time. In the listing for dealing the least deals, which is a great disadvantage; for that makes the Dealer youngest hand.

The Dealer deals out two to the first hand, and turns up to the third, and so goes on to the next, to the third, fourth, fifth, &c. He that has the biggest card carries the Bone, that is, one half of the Stake, the other remaining for the game; now if there be three Kings, three Queens, three tens, &c. turned up, the eldest hand wins it. Here note, that the Ace of Diamonds is *Bone-Ace*, and wins all other cards whatever. Thus much for the Bone; afterwards the nearest to one and thirty wins the game, and he that turns up, or draws to one and thirty, wins it immediately.

CHARLES COTTON
WIT and REASON, a Game so called.
from The Compleat Gamester (1674)

WIT and REASON is a game which seems very easy at first to the learner, but in his practice and observation shall find it otherwise. It is a game something like one and thirty, and is played after this manner.

Two playing together, the one has all the red Cards, and the other has the black: then they turn up, cross or pile, who shall lead; for the Leader has a great advantage over the other, as shall be demonstrated.

You are not to play a Ten first; for if you do you shall certainly lose; for one and thirty, being the game, he that first comes to it wins; now should the Leader play a Ten, the Follower will play another Ten, that makes twenty; let the Leader then play any thing next, the Follower will be sure to make it up one and thirty.

He that hath the lead, if he play a Nine, may certainly win the game, if he look about him; ever remembering to get first to twenty, without spending two of one sort, as two Deuces, two Treys, two Quaters, &c. otherwise you will lose: As for example, you play a Nine first, your Adversary plays a Deuce that makes eleven, you play a Nine again, and that makes twenty; thus you have played but both your Nines, wherefore your Antagonist plays a Deuce, now you can play no card but he wins; for if you play an eight (for you cannot come in with your Ten) and you have never a Nine, then he has an Ace for one and thirty; so if you play a Seven, which makes Nine and Twenty, he has a Deuce remaining to make up one and thirty, and so you may observe in the rest of the cards.

Take this for a general rule, that you have a very great advantage in fetching out, by play, any two of a number, as aforesaid; as two Fives, two Sixes, two Sevens, &c. wherefore you must not play rashly, but with due consideration arithmetically grounded to make up a certain game of one and thirty. To conclude, he that hath the art of playing well at One and Thirty, with cards, that is, by naming such a number at first, and prosecuting it by such Addition of others, that your Adversary cannot think of any Number but what shall be your Game; I say such a man is fittest to play at this Game called *WIT and REASON*.

H. G. WELLS
Little Wars
from Little Wars: A Game for Boys
from twelve years of age to one hundred and fifty
and for that more intelligent sort of girl
who likes boys' games and books (1913)

HERE, then, are the rules of the perfect battle-game as we play it in an ordinary room.

THE COUNTRY

(1) The Country must be arranged by one player, who, failing any other agreement, shall be selected by the toss of a coin.

(2) The other player shall then choose which side of the field he will fight from.

(3) The Country must be disturbed as little as possible in each move. Nothing in the Country shall be moved or set aside deliberately to facilitate the firing of guns. A player must not lie across the Country so as to crush or disturb the Country if his opponent objects. Whatever is moved by accident shall be replaced after the end of the move.

THE MOVE

(1) After the Country is made and the sides chosen, then (and not until then) the players shall toss for the first move.

(2) If there is no curtain, the player winning the toss, hereafter called the First Player, shall next arrange his men along his back line, as he chooses. Any men he may place behind or in front of his back line shall count in the subsequent move as if they touched the back line at its nearest point. The Second Player shall then do the same. But if a curtain is available both first and second player may put down their men at the same time. Both players may take unlimited time for the putting down of their men; if there is a curtain it is drawn back when they are ready, and the game then begins.

GILES GOODLAND
Psyche and Erosion

Use tab to open box, remove packaging and reflective suit. Use the full pack of 52 paintbrushes to outline legs, then the lookup table to interpolate corrected values, and unwrap the Sword of Names. Arm movements strike capitals, grab claws lay hold of limbs, and mechanical paws stroke wound areas. Remember to use event-trees to represent yesterday operators on your board. Your opponent is your soul.

Use the dotted line to trace paths of sprawling events and muted watercolours to draw your bodiless opponent: as you do this, use velcro to keep spycam attached, use a waterpot with its body buried in your future grave; maintain an icy blue calm using a harlequin pattern. Show your thinking by use of block capitals: the resulting neural network diagram may indicate your soul's location.

Being sure to position your earphones, use an ifstatement without elsebranch while using deck relation to declare symbol use. Next, use XML-based format to store events; use the Sternberg memory task and inflight effects to spend your cooldown: let hourglass hits and audio queues feedback while deploying either fixed or fluxed harms. Imitate the calls of insects. Use wicked and uncanny ways to create potential wells: use gentle cycle for maximum fluffiness or use fake to daze your adversary.

If the task requires you to design a compliant solid-state armament with editing capability, use a reamer to enlarge hole so it fits leg taper; then use a gutter adze to rough out the blade. Build a many-hued paradise from bricks, install within it your pheromone trap. Lure into it your Psyche. Use the pebble-count to list bed-and-bank material, remembering that different voices are used to address: dogs, toddlers, partners, the very old, the dead, gods, God. You may use the Ode form, but not the vocative.

Your opponent is both subtle and double. Choose subtitle or dub modes. An elseblock node before cleanup in a finally block to control searches at instance start time. Use double duchesse silk chine to stiffen excessive folds and particle -swarms to optimise joint angle; erect an 11-storey decoy apartment building using foldcrete; use compatible screw patterns with regulate mount; the expense fund screen will fence your gains. Entrap your soul in one of three genie bottles. Guess which.

Your soul will arise as a djinn. Use forward slash to hack opponent, backslash to lash yourself. Use DS statement to set aside silos for warheads: use columns from your insertion point onward for phosphor storage and a TV camera readout system to add to a sprite using perspective warp; use if instruction to check that the number of sprites loading is larger than 0. Utilise red-dot or in-sight.

Deal. Place your cards as bookmarks in your dog-eared Proust (Scott Moncrieff translation): aces count high in chapters with analepsis, and low where prolepsis occurs; then use ogive as hybrid target bullets in one of two general strategies to degrade metadata. Use ace 2 3 4 5 6 for the runners, for playing tos and fros use x and y axes to adjust pitch and yaw; fill background with paintbucket drawing three-lane highway incoporating fake tunnel entrance; first create an animated character to trick opponent into turning off smartphone.

By using sonnet to celebrate your perfections you underplay your rival: six rhymes should be used, the hourglass, or king kansu, being eliminated. Play the king when a number over two cancels the first three joystick functions in initialisation at max nodes. Use generalised threats to prevent Left from losing if Right plays first; use it to silence a room of losers. Your soul will be among them.

To signal the end of the outdoor phase use sardines on retreat to terrify a group of high guys executing a raid. Souls feed on love: they predate you. Use your noose to manoeuvre a carried broadsword into the dragon, then drop it to unlock or lock a door, move a carried key of the right colour into it. Use sense or innocence, but not subsense. Separate soul from body, if not already sundered.

If you have got this far, describe your experience (use only grammatical forms not previously used: for instance, prepositional pronouns). Introspection is the most effective weapon here: use inwit to outwit. Email or post your account to your only surviving primary school teacher.

You should by now be a decade older. Locate on your body: soil creep, sump detritus, weeping wells. Use your psychotic laugh to close. Heads win, for now. Replace in box.

CAMILLE RALPHS
She Plays the Box Game

[*Stark lighting, casting shadows under chins, noses and words.* SHE *sits, stage left. Beside: a line of ten seats, each one occupied by someone else.* SHE *and the others all hold boxes.*]

SHE: What have you got in your box?
ONE: [*opening the box*] The top of the morning.
SHE: Looks like a spinning top to me. Next!
[ONE *leaves*; SHE *moves up to* TWO.]
SHE: What have you got in your box?
TWO: [*opening the box*] A fairy tale.
SHE: Looks like a cat o' nine tails to me. Next!
[TWO *leaves;* SHE *moves up to* THREE.]
SHE: What have you got in your box?
THREE: [*opening the box*] A horn of plenty.
SHE: Looks like an air horn to me. Next!
[THREE *leaves*; SHE *moves up to* FOUR.]
SHE: What have you got in your box?
FOUR: [*opening the box*] The name of the game.
SHE: Looks like a pseudonym to me. Next!
[FOUR *leaves;* SHE *moves up to* FIVE.]
SHE: What have you got in your box?
FIVE: [*opening the box*] A magic trick.
SHE: Looks like a trick of the light to me. Next!
[FIVE *leaves;* SHE *moves up to* SIX.]
SHE: What have you got in your box?

SIX: [*opening the box*] The third eye.
SHE: Looks like the eye of the storm to me. Next!
[SIX *leaves;* SHE *moves up to* SEVEN.]
SHE: What have you got in your box?
SEVEN: [*opening the box*] The world tree.
SHE: Looks like a gallows tree to me. Next!
[SEVEN *leaves;* SHE *moves up to* EIGHT.]
SHE: What have you got in your box?
EIGHT: [*opening the box*] The key to all mythologies.
SHE: Looks like keyhole surgery to me. Next!
[EIGHT *leaves;* SHE *moves up to* NINE.]
SHE: What have you got in your box?
NINE: [opening the box] The road back.
SHE: Looks like a back road to me. Next!
[NINE *leaves;* SHE *moves up to* TEN.]
SHE: What have you got in your box?
TEN: [*opening the box*] A red flag.
SHE: [*Pauses, shocked*] Yes . . . Yes, it's a red flag!
I adore your honesty.
TEN: What have you got in your box?
SHE: The same.
TEN: [*Opens her box. A white flag shows itself.*]
I see. Looks like surrender to me.

CURTAIN

Stakeout

Perch by an upper-floor window.
Follow the dazed stagger of a raindrop on glass.
Keep perfectly still.
Bogart a punnet of something.
Scissor a recipe from the newspaper.
Go out.
Goof off.
Gaslight yourself a little.
Pause to talk to a hedge-bird.
Kick through husky yellow leaves.
Pretend you're reading a softcore love scene.
Count three different kinds of uniform.
Kiss the back of your hand.
Lay it on your hot cheek.
Eastwood a tree stump.
Hang a pair of binoculars from your neck.
Dictate a letter to whomever is tailing you.
Install a new piece of software.
Invent a new kind of insect.
Wait a while at the midpoint of a bridge.
Take a long and lazy swim.
Dry yourself with your underwear.
MacGyver a swingseat.
Make promises. What harm can a promise do?
Keep your footsteps as soft as you can.

Imagine you're flying a small private plane.
Smash up some ice.
Write down your idea for a TV show.
Leave a door ajar.
Softsoap the shopkeep.
Get waylaid.
Get woolly-headed.
Make your own blacklist.
Come home early.
Mothball a bathmat.
Cradle the instruction manual anxiously.
Unhair thy oxters.
Return to the window.
Answer a soft question or two.
Wear your dressing gown half-off.
Dream about life on the river.
Bail out a boat in the dream.
Give a name to a cat that isn't yours.
Wear your dressing gown barely-on.
Turn over an hourglass.
Especially do not feign affection.
Hogtie a soft toy.
Untie the soft toy.
Hash out a list of instructions.
Go, wiser thou! and, in thy scale of sense,
say goodnight.
Have a good night's sleep.

Incomplete or ambiguous games are most familiar to us in the context of fiction. In stories of distant worlds or secret societies, strange contests with only partially-defined rules are used to suggest alternate social traditions, values and rituals. They are typically presented as opportunities for a protagonist to either develop or demonstrate an intimate understanding of an alien culture. Often, however, the authors of these stories rely on pronounced similarities to games familiar to their readers, partly to avoid long-winded explanations and partly, one would think, because it's difficult to conceive of a game unlike one which already exists.

By way of example, in Edgar Rice Burroughs' 1922 novel *Chessmen of Mars*, the Barsoomian game of Jetan is based heavily on chess – only played on a larger (10 x 10) chequered board with more pieces. This obvious kinship has allowed Burroughs' readers to recreate Jetan, and even improve on its rules, outside of the confines of the novel. Other attempts by audiences to translate fictional games into real ones have met with varying degrees of success – some are passion projects, others commercial ventures. The challenge posed is similar to that faced by archaeologists hoping to reconstruct the rules to ancient games which have survived only as engraved wooden or stone boards: the Mesopotamian 'Royal Game of Ur', for instance, or the Egyptian games of Senet and Mehen, the latter of which involves moving carved pieces across the segments of a coiled snake.

Other games, such as mahjong and backgammon, have persisted long enough for multiple variants on their rules and components to emerge. All of these examples serve to remind us that although they impose restrictions and bind us to arbitrary goals, games are primarily combinations of objects and ideas that serve an expressive purpose; that is, we play them in order to act out roles, to inhabit different ways of being, of seeing and of understanding.

CLIFF HAMMETT

Tempo

(Time-based chess variants)

Tempo is a set of unstable chess variants that plays with the ways in which time operates in the game. Each variant brings in forces and capabilities normally excluded from the game of chess – for better or worse. The turn structure of chess is disrupted, either by allowing turns out of sequence, or even multiple turns at once, destabilising the game and opening questions of how its rules now apply. Each variant is less a functioning game, more an exercise in thinking through how games operate, and their limits and potentials as models of social, economic and ecological situations.

All versions require a complete chess set, as well as further equipment set out below. Some variants are far more active than ordinary chess, so make sure you are in a space where it is safe to move and run around.

CALCULATED CALORIES CHESS

Burn a set number of calories before taking a turn.

WHAT YOU NEED:
A device that can estimate calories burned through physical activity, such as a FitBit or cheap heart-rate monitor.

HOW IT WORKS:
Decide how many calories you and your opponent will need to burn before taking a move. The amount does not have to be the same for each player; you can vary it based on your physical capacities, energy levels or your confidence at playing chess. You can make it fair, comically unfair or difficult to predict. Begin – jog on the spot, jump around or sit back and let the calories fall off through intense consideration of your next move. Once your device says you have burned sufficient calories, take your turn. It might be that one player takes several turns before the other. Work with it.

PARTY CHESS

Earn chaotic sequences of moves by inflating a balloon and using it to sound a whistle.

WHAT YOU NEED:
Two balloon pumps, two balloons and two party whistles.

HOW IT WORKS:
You and your opponent are each equipped with a balloon, a pump, and a party whistle. You must inflate the balloon and attach it to your party whistle in order to start taking turns. While the whistle is sounding, you may continually take moves, one after the other. Once the whistle has stopped, you must stop taking moves and pump up the balloon once

more. Make the most of your brief moment of power – your opponent's chance may be mere seconds away.

TIMER CHESS

A way of including people who may not wish to play themselves, or who find it challenging to play the above variants. Combine with another variant for best results.

WHAT YOU NEED:
An easily resettable timer.

HOW IT WORKS:
It's very simple. Set a timer to an agreed period, and start it going. Once this time has elapsed, take a turn then reset the timer. This pairs best with Calculated Calories Chess; if combined with Party Chess, you may wish to give a very small amount of time between turns.

BALLOON CHESS CRICKET

An adaptation of Party Chess for four players.

WHAT YOU NEED:
Two balloon pumps, two balloons, and two friends to serve as fielders, one for you and one for your opponent.

HOW IT WORKS:
In order to take moves, you and your opponent must inflate your balloons once more. This time, instead of attaching the balloon to a whistle, release it into the air. You can then take as many moves as you want, until your opponent's fielder catches the said balloon, shouts "OUT" (or any word that amuses you) and returns the balloon to you.

MAKE YOUR OWN

Once you have tried a few of these variants, why not try inventing your own version? Perhaps you'll want to stabilise the game to make it more playable, or seek new and interesting ways to cause the game to collapse. You could try applying these approaches to other games. Maybe you will pursue whole new directions. Whatever you decide, have fun!

CAPTAIN A. S. HARRISON
Knuckle Bones

The game is played with five bones, and the stages are as follows:

1. *Beginnings.* The five bones are gathered in the palm of the hand and thrown up, any number being caught on the back of the hand; they are then tossed up again, and caught in the palm. One is selected, thrown into the air, and one at a time the remainder picked up, while the one thrown is in the air. This must be caught and again thrown for the next bone. The bone thrown up is called the 'dab,' and must be caught clear, without touching any part of the person but the right hand under all circumstances of the game.

2. *Ones.* The five bones are thrown on to the table, and the dab selected is thrown up, and the remainder are taken up, one by one, without touching any other bone.

3. *Twos.* The same again, but two taken up for each throw of the dab.

4. *Threes.* Three picked up, and then one.

5. *Fours.* Four picked up.

In twos, threes, and fours, it is permitted by consent of the adversary to push the selected bones together while the dab is in the air. The touching of any other than the selected bones, or the failure to pick up the proper number, forfeits the turn.

6. *Short Spans.* Two bones are placed on the table, each side of the left hand, one pair close to the thumb, the other pair at the tip of the little finger. Each pair must be taken up separately, without any pushing together.

7. *Long Spans.* A bone is placed at the extremities of the thumb and little finger, stretched out to the widest. Another pair is put in the same way about six inches farther on the table. These pairs must be taken up without any touching together: any bone displaced may be put back again three times; failure on the third trial forfeits the turn.

8. *Creek Mouse.* The five bones are tossed from the palm, and any number caught on the back of the hand; all but one are shaken off; the remainder are then gathered into the palm, without disturbing the one on the back, which is then tossed and caught in the palm, with the others.

9. *Second Creek Mouse.* The five bones are tossed from the palm as before, and one is retained on the back. The remainder are taken one between each finger and thumb, the one on the back is then tossed and caught in the extended palm.

10. *Bridges.* The hand is laid on the back on the table, the bones held between the fingers are then dropped in a row on the table. An arch is formed with the first finger and thumb of the left hand at about six inches from the left-hand bone of the four. They are then one by one pushed through this bridge; when all are through the left hand is removed, and the four are taken up at one sweep. No touching together is allowed.

11. *Cracks.* The bones are thrown on the table, and the four picked up one by one; the dab in falling and being caught to make a distinct crack on the one picked up.

12. *No Cracks.* Same as before, but the dab must be caught without touching the other bone. The slightest sound forfeits the turn.

13. *Exchanges.* The four bones are laid at the corners of a square, a full span on each side. The first bone is picked up from the lower right-hand corner, and at the next throw is exchanged for the one above. This is exchanged for the one at the top left-hand corner, this for the lower left, and that is placed at the point of starting. The bones are then taken up in diagonal pairs.

14. *Everlastings.* The whole of the bones are tossed from the palms, and any number caught on the back. These are tossed from the back and caught in the palm; and any that have fallen in the first toss have to be picked up while the

whole of the others are in the air, so that at one moment there may be four dabs and one to pick up. This task, as the name implies, approaches the everlasting.

The game is an excellent one for exercising and developing that perfect sympathy between the eye and the hand which is certain to be of great service in after life.

ASTRA PAPACHRISTODOULOU
Shouty Full Moon

This game will trick your friends into thinking that the moon is mad at them for no apparent reason. As a result, they will be confused and too terrified to look at the night sky while the moon is bright. Please only play this prank on friends you despise – it's harmless, but it acts as sweet revenge for those who've annoyed you in one way or another. It could be someone who always turns up late at your annual Gollum-themed pyjama party or the kind of 'friend' who borrows one of your Bob Cobbing books and never returns it! You will also need a chair (ideally silver-coloured), various party props and a full moon.

HOW TO PLAY:
First, buy or make your own moon costume. Make sure its surface is as realistic as possible. Next, throw a murder mystery party and invite your most annoying friends. Before the party starts, hide both your moon costume and the chair somewhere close to a direct view of the moon, e.g. behind the curtains of a large window or a back-garden bush. At the end of the final round of the murder mystery, when the moon is at its brightest, ask the attendees to assemble around your hiding place for the reveal of the murderer.

While they are distracted, change into your moon costume and arrange your chair in front of the real moon. Stand on the chair. Turn off any electric lights so that everyone is bewildered. Now hold your nose as you speak, dramatically altering the sound of your voice. Start shouting the kind of insults that the moon would use, were it a person. No swearing is required – be as creative as possible with your harmless little slights. Everyone will be puzzled as to why the moon is shouting at them. At the pinnacle of your performance, reveal your real identity and watch everyone's jaws drop in slow motion. A perfect ending to what will hopefully be a very entertaining night of mystery and drama!

UNKNOWN
Hot Cockles

A game not unlike Shadow Buff is that known by the peculiar title of Hot Cockles. A handkerchief is tied over the eyes of one of the company, who then lays his head on a chair, as if he were about to submit to the punishment of being beheaded, and places his hand on his back with the palm uppermost. Any of the party come behind him and give him a slap on his open hand, he in the meantime trying to discover whose hand it is that strikes.

UNKNOWN
I apprenticed my son

The shortest way of describing this game will be to give an illustration of the manner in which it is played.

John: "I apprenticed my son to a grocer, and the first thing he sold was half-a-pound of C."

Nellie: Coffee?—No.

Sam: Cocoa?—No.

Tom: Cayenne Pepper?—No.

Edith: Chicory?—Yes.

Edith being the guesser of the right article, is entitled to be the next to apprentice her son. One guess only in turn is allowed to each player.

KATE GREENAWAY

Shouting Proverbs

from Kate Greenaway's Book of Games (1889)

One player leaves the room and the others choose a proverb, of which they each take a word. The absent player having been recalled, at a given signal everyone shouts simultaneously his or her own word, by which means the proverb must be guessed.

KATE GREENAWAY

Queen Anne and Her Maids

from Kate Greenaway's Book of Games (1889)

One player covers her eyes, while the others, standing in a row close to each other, put their hands behind them. One has a ball concealed, which all pretend to have. They then call the one who has covered her eyes, and addressing her sing:

> *Queen Anne, Queen Anne, she sits in the sun;*
> *As fair as a lily, as brown as a bun;*
> *She sends you three letters, and begs you'll read one!*

To which Queen Anne replies:

> *I cannot read one unless I read seven,*
> *So please, my assassin, surrender your weapon.*

She then extends an open palm in the direction of the person she thinks has the ball. If she has guessed correctly, the assassin takes Queen Anne's place. If it was a wrong guess she hides her eyes again while the ball changes hands, returning as a different queen.

Conundra

Players are sent out of the room while someone hides a thimble (or other small object) in a place where it can be seen. The players are then called in to discover it. They may not displace or open anything, and should carry out their search without speaking, giving the task their total attention. As each one lays eyes on the thimble, they must (without giving away its position) act the part of one whose mind has been eased, who has had their life and all its fussy pleasures restored to them all at once. They may talk, drink, be jolly. The person who first sees it hides it next time.

Medusa

An inversion of *Conundra*. The object is again placed where it can be seen, as well as within easy reach. When the players return their purpose is to locate it without so much as glimpsing it. They may not close or shield their eyes, nor stare straight up at the ceiling. Any who do see the object must freeze completely until either it is discovered by touch, or all players have been petrified.

In the design of simulation-style tabletop games (where the steps of the game are directly analagous to real-world situations and choices) there is a powerful tendency to cast the player as a person of high rank or social status. In chess, as in nearly all war games, the player is given command of an army, while in Monopoly they begin with the funds to invest in property. Ordinary people, in the context of these games, are reduced to units or do not exist at all; it appears that in simplified models of the world, very few of us have agency.

Is the entire point, in such cases, to allow us to indulge in a fantasy of power and significance? Better, perhaps, to think of them as exercising a kind of muscle. Much of our lives may be governed by rules that are kept hidden from us and decisions made without our consultation, but there is a pressing need to be ready for, and alert to, those occasions when our choices have far-reaching consequences, for others as well as ourselves.

ROB WALTON

Mittball

(A role-playing game for two players)

Equipment: baseball, baseball mitt, well-stocked cocktail cabinet, two adjoining rooms.

Whichever of you is the best Steve McQueen lookalike should be shut in one room by themselves, having incurred the wrath of the prison camp guards.

'McQueen' should wear the baseball mitt on their left hand and hold the baseball in their right hand. While in the room, they should repeatedly bounce the ball against the wall/floor and catch it. It is this player's responsibility to keep a count of the successful/successive bounce/catches. The target is 76.

The other player, the guard, should take position by the cocktail cabinet in the other room and pour themselves a glass of port or fino sherry and sip it slowly. They should then attempt to make a snowball from scratch and add a glacé cherry. They should aim to raise the glass and say "Cheers!" before the other player reaches their target.

CONWENNA RAY

Spicebush Silkmoth

from Micro Machines *(1921)*

The mouths of adult *Callosamia promethea* are vestigial, she says. They cannot eat. They live for only a week. During that time they mate in the late afternoon and evening, for an hour or more at a time. The females are nocturnal and polyandrous, the males diurnal and polygamous – meaning they both seek out as many partners as possible.

Do you want to play the spicebush silkmoth game? I say that I doubt I would be very good at it. You don't have to mate with anyone, she says. It's pretend. It's a game about noticing and deepening our connections to others.

Explain to me how it works, then, I say. You have one week, she says. You score a point for spending half an hour or more in another person's company after 4pm each day. You don't have to talk much, but you ought to be aware of one another, and you must, at some point, touch something of theirs with something of yours – a clinking of glasses, a crossing of papers, a brief butting of shoes.

She demonstrates by tapping my fork with hers.

You can only score one point per person, even if you see them again the next day. You can also only score one point per half hour – so if you go out with a group, it is as if you were with only one of them for the first thirty minutes, another one for the second thirty minutes, and so on.

And that's it? I say.

There is another way of increasing your score, she says. You can add on the score of any of your partners – if you're able to find out what it is.

So they would have to be playing the game too, I say.

Not necessarily. You can explain the rules to them, and they may be able to tell you what their score would be, in the event that they *were* playing the game. This is a risky move, of course.

Does this really deepen our connection to others? I say. She shrugs.

Perhaps the point is that it makes you ask yourself that. Your mouth, by the way, is fully operational, and you may eat as much as you like throughout the week. But at the end, you die, and your wings – I don't know if you've ever seen a silkmoth, but the wings are very large. Folded back they're like big, stylish pompadours. Anyway, your wings will wilt as if they were cabbage leaves or a burning bathrobe.

The Scavenger God

Go now, and collect the following moods or expressions by reading them in people's faces – in the way they screw up their eyes, in the tint of their cheeks or the bunching of their brows. When you recognise one, take a mental picture, then cross it off your list. Take as long as you need – hours, days, weeks – but gather *ten* of them.

☐ Embattlement / ☐ Vigorous admiration / ☐ Pure, white-hot excitement / ☐ Faltering confidence / ☐ Tremulous joy / ☐ Coiled fatigue / ☐ Wild disapppointment / ☐ A dry sort of disgust / ☐ Taut apprehension / ☐ Strained interest / ☐ Intense interest / ☐ Uncomprehending sorrow / ☐ Fast-encroaching discomfort / ☐ Uncertainty / ☐ Momentary aloofness / ☐ An almost imperceptible twitch of vexation / ☐ Satisfaction / ☐ Dissatisfaction / ☐ Subdued surprise / ☐ A polite sham of frenzied pleasure / ☐ Glumness / ☐ Creeping arrogance / ☐ Rancid boredom / ☐ Cool determination / ☐ Indelicate zeal / ☐ Mischievosity / ☐ Shock / ☐ Burgeoning tenderness / ☐ Splendid rage / ☐ Shimmering desire / ☐ Exasperation / ☐ Serenity

Once you've checked off ten, it's time to return to your workshop, and to the two humanoid automata you've been building there. Their names are Harriet and Henry, and all that's required in order for them to be whole is that they be imbued with personality. You must therefore divide those moods and expressions you've collected between them – five for one, five for the other. This will define the range of emotions of which each is capable.

Now, stand back, and behold your creations!

/

This game may be replayed using different names for the robots:

Suze and Dave • Thelma and Louise • Ginger and Lacey • Geraldine and Jean • Jonathan and Simon • Momo and Kimiko • Robobill and Robobert • Midnight and Noon • Stuff and Nonsense • Peaches and Cream • Sugar and Lemon • Dolly and Candy • Upstairs and Downstairs • Sapphire and Steel • Ticket and Punch • Bundle and Scram • Rhapsody and Harmony • Empire and Wasteland • Sizzle and Guzzle • Mum and Dad • Doom and Dread • Angel and Angel • Animal and Man

CHARLOTTE HEATHER
Chronic Illness: The Tabletop RPG

The main mechanic of this game is the feedback loop of energy use. You'll be given five spoons to place in front of you. Do not question the spoons.

In this game you get what you're given.

Each action costs you one spoon.

Actions you may take include, but are not limited to: *fighting running problem-solving walking talking eating screwing loving digesting crying sleeping sitting shitting breathing*

To reach the next level, make sure you take plenty of rest breaks. To take rest breaks you must be supine, succumb to gravity, thinking of nothing.

You must also use designated restorative spots, or 'beds'.

Each time you find a 'bed', roll a dice to determine the quality of your rest. The number you roll determines how many spoons you will receive.

You may think this game seems difficult. It is. You play the role you are given.

True, the next adventure looks much like the one before that and the one before that and the one before that and the one before that and the one before that, ad infinitum.

How can you win?
That's really beside the point.

Library on Fire

This game takes a minute to play – since you should never spend longer than a minute in a library on fire.

Yes, the library is on fire.

It is a private library – really, a kind of trophy room. It contains a large number of rare texts: works by Euclid, Agricola, Volta. *The Birds of America*, *La Palla di Neve*, The Book of August, the Codex Cubiculum, *Celestine*, *The Oyster*. Manuscripts, incunables and first-edition Ulva Undreamts.

The owner has gone mad and set it all ablaze (this was always on the cards). You must save as many books as you can, but discerningly, while the flames fall upon their banquet.

To play, open any nearby book on a random page and, as you start a 60-second timer, place your finger on a word of your choosing (this represents you seizing on a promising shelf). To start gathering books, make new words (of two letters or more) by rearranging the letters of your starter word. IMPORTANT: *Each new word you make cannot have more letters than the previous word, since you shouldn't stack a bigger book on top of a smaller one.*

EXAMPLE: The player chooses the starter word 'preceding'. They write down, in this order, 'creeping', 'pincered', 'pierced', 'ceding', 'cinder', 'rind', 'cede', 'dine', 'din' and 'in'.

They have rescued ten books (the starter word does not count). If they can go no further and there's time left, they can pick a new starter word and make another stack. Once the 60 seconds are over, they must abandon the library.

SINGLE-PLAYER SCORING:
2-6: Most of what you've hauled from the fire can be found in any antiquarian bookshop.
7-10: You emerge with some warmed-over volumes on horology and mesmerism.
11-14: Among these are the only surviving works of an early *zhiguai xiaoshuo* author.
15-16: You've picked up a grimoire which bleeds blue smoke!
17-18: One of your finds is a lost play of Agathon!
18-20: Every one of these is one of a kind.
20+: Scholars will journey from across the world for centuries to examine this lightly scorched bundle of volumes.

MULTIPLAYER VARIATION

Instead of adding up a total, you each must describe the most valuable book you managed to save. To do this, make a title out of only the words you have written down, and explain what this work entails. Using the words from the previous example, the player announces they've retrieved a late-19th-century gothic horror reworking of the Cinderella folk story, called *Creeping Cinder*.

Near Dogluck Weir

A bashful day, a sultry day slackening – but only just. Much sagging on the riverbank. The river blinks its hundred shears. Two gorgeous swimmers race to the bridge and back, while their gorgeous friend watches from the shade.

You are either (in a one-player game) the Gorgeous Friend, or (in a two-player game) one of the swimmers, whom we shall call the Gorgeous Girl and the Gorgeous Boy.

Roll a die to determine the result of the race, with the first roll determining who starts (evens: Gorgeous Girl, odds: Gorgeous Boy). Subsequent rolls advance each swimmer in turn across the board (opposite and following pages). If you are playing the Friend, you roll for both.

Some of the places on the board have accompanying descriptive text for you to read, and instructions in italics for each of the players to follow.

The surface's cut cloth rucks.
Girl, kick your legs until the next roll lands.

She sheds the river as if
it were one unending shift.

GIRL BEGIN ◯—◯—◯—◯—⑤—◯—◯—◯—

All hold your breath until the game ends.

And where there was her, •••••••••• �65—◯—◯—◯—
there is a heron.

He becomes a green shadow, •••••••• �65—◯—◯—◯—
a pike.

All stretch out until the game ends.

BOY BEGIN ◯—◯—◯—◯—⑤—◯—◯—◯—

His flesh busy fizzling like oil in a pan.

Cider surge. Studded anklets.
Friend/Boy, hold your breath until the next roll lands.

81

Ripsaw at the river's waist. White splinters!
Friend, take a flash photo of yourself.

Sun splits its axe upon her haunch.
Girl, writhe a little. Move forward three.

Hot rent in the river's fuselage.
*Friend/Girl, imagine you're broken
in two, both halves drifting.*

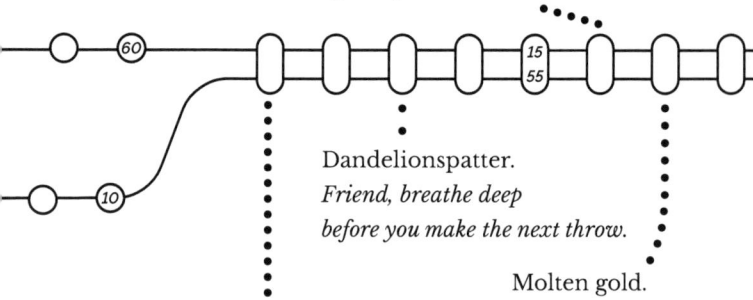

All: close your eyes until the next throw lands.

Dandelionspatter.
*Friend, breathe deep
before you make the next throw.*

Molten gold.
*Boy, roll again.
Friend, take off /
put on your socks.
Adjust your glasses.*

Hammer in the forge, sunken coins.
*Boy, recall a taste of metal and wine.
Choose a word for it.*

(SWIMMERS MAY NOT OVERTAKE ONE ANOTHER ON THIS PAGE)

Motley of conjuror's silks, suddenly whipped away. But...!
Swimmers: if you are both on this page, swap positions.

The reek of the river:
loose keen and lizardly.
*All: pretend to be eating
a nectarine
straight off the branch.*

Iron shadow
of the bridge, astride
the river's hips.
*All: think of a small, dark,
private spot.*

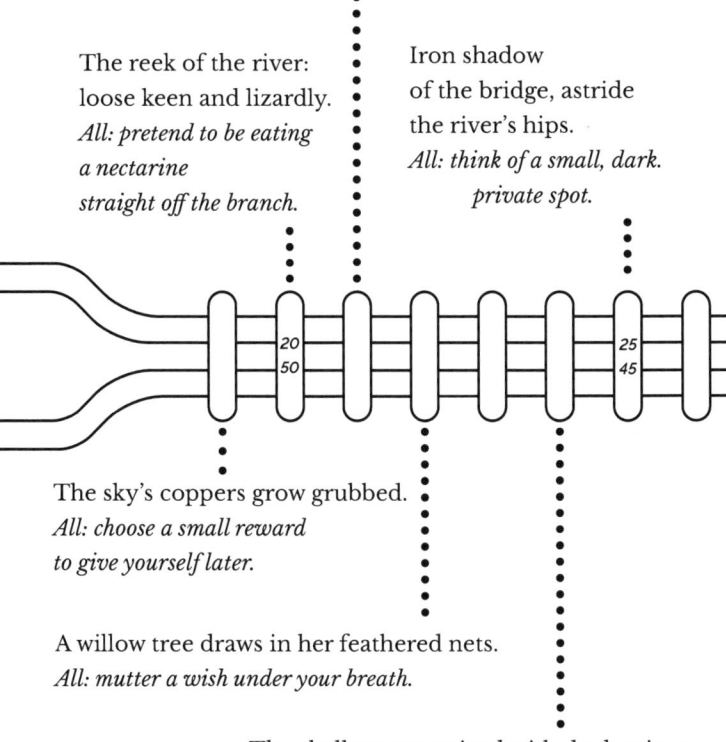

The sky's coppers grow grubbed.
*All: choose a small reward
to give yourself later.*

A willow tree draws in her feathered nets.
All: mutter a wish under your breath.

The shallows are spiced with duck mites.
Boy/Girl: roll for your opponent's next turn.

83

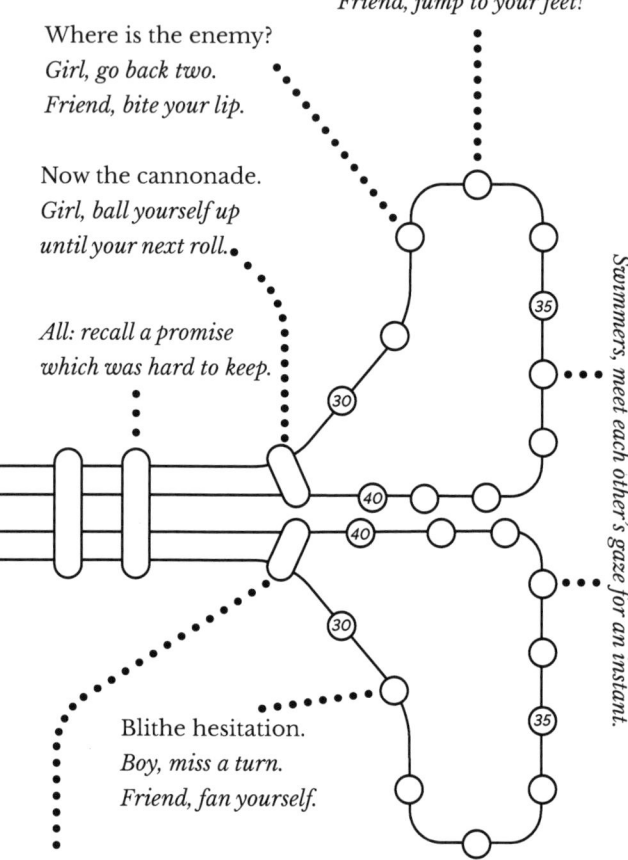

Her body like a harpoon, wounding the water.
Friend, jump to your feet!

Where is the enemy?
Girl, go back two.
Friend, bite your lip.

Now the cannonade.
Girl, ball yourself up
until your next roll.

All: recall a promise
which was hard to keep.

Swimmers, meet each other's gaze for an instant.

Blithe hesitation.
Boy, miss a turn.
Friend, fan yourself.

GO, TORPEDOBOY!
Boy, close your eyes tight and hold your breath
until your next dice roll.

Paper Date

(A Dicey Dating Sim)

Charlie is ravishing and tanned. Frankie is an ice-cool intellectual. Jamie is a slim, smooth enigma. Will you land a date with any of them? Can you send a solitary shiver through a single one?

This game is played over a number of rounds, each corresponding to an encounter with one of this trio of potential paramours. The round starts with a roll of the die to decide which of the three you've contrived to run into:

1-2: Charlie • 3-4: Frankie • 5-6: Jamie

Next, choose a number between 0 and 2. This represents how big a chance you're willing to take. Do you tend toward caution, or are you ready to make a serious move, should the opportunity arise?

Roll the die again, and add the number on the die to the one you've chosen, giving you a total between 1 and 8. Use the TABLES in the next section to find out how this figure affects your *Rapport* and *Electricity* stats. You have a different set for each potential date, so that's six stats in total to keep track of. If you want to play the game on *Easy Mode*, your starting stat for each is 4. If you want to play on *Hard Mode* it's 2, and if you want to play on *Real Life Mode* it's 0.

Once you have adjusted your stats, the round is complete and you can move on to the next.

Your stats cannot fall below 0. If you incur a negative penalty for a stat already at 0, you have (I'm sorry to say) crashed and burned – that relationship is now irrecoverable. Ignore future dice rolls suggesting an encounter with this character.

If both your *Rapport* and *Electricity* stats for the same character reach 10 or more, you have won that character over completely and may start drawing up plans for a very entertaining evening.

1. TABLES

A meeting with Charlie

If a total of ↴
1: You appear to Charlie as a dour, distracted writer, muttering *books, books, books*.
-4 ELECTRICITY/-2 RAPPORT
2: You appear to Charlie as a rough-lipped, rough-tongued gardener, wearing the mildest shimmer of sweat-glow.
+3 ELECTRICITY/+4 RAPPORT
3-4: You appear to Charlie as a silver harlequin.
 +3 RAPPORT/-3 ELECTRICITY
5-6: You appear to Charlie as a detective in a switchblade suit.
+2 ELECTRICITY/-1 RAPPORT

7: You appear to Charlie as a thing of pure dream, all maelstrom-eyes and burning wings:
+4 ELECTRICITY/+4 RAPPORT
8: You appear to Charlie as a monstrous cloud, cackling mad, dark spells.
+6 ELECTRICITY/-6 RAPPORT

A meeting with Frankie

If a total of ↴
1: You talk to Frankie about [oenology / ethnobotany / foxing]
+14 RAPPORT
2: You talk to Frankie about [prop making / extreme ironing / urban planning].
-1 ELECTRICITY/-1 RAPPORT
3-4: You talk to Frankie about [Charlie and Jamie / your cooking / Dr. Crippen].
-2 RAPPORT
5-6: You talk to Frankie about [fleshy excrescences / comedy / Kazuo Ishiguro].
-2 ELECTRICITY
7: You talk to Frankie about [your fanfiction / children / neoplatonism]:
-1 ELECTRICITY/-1 RAPPORT
8: You talk to Frankie about [deep sea organisms / D. H. Lawrence's 'clitoral' mushrooms / robotics].
+14 ELECTRICITY

A meeting with Jamie

If a total of ↴

1: You sit delicately opposite one another, tethered to your coffee cups.
-2 ELECTRICITY/+2 RAPPORT

2: You circle one another in the library, choose similar anthologies.
-1 ELECTRICITY/+1 to RAPPORT

3-4: You walk through the same mossy forest.
+1 RAPPORT

5-6: You eat lunch together in the cemetery.
+1 ELECTRICITY/-1 RAPPORT

7: You both miss your train. -1 ELECTRICITY

8: You brush a bare strip of Jamie with a bare swatch of you.
+12 ELECTRICITY/-8 RAPPORT

2. KEEPING TRACK OF YOUR STATS

Use pencil and paper. Write down –

Rapport w. C:
Elec. w. C:
Rapport w. F:
Elec. w. F:
Rapport w. J:
Elec. w. J:

Fill in your starting stats (4, 2 or 0, depending on difficulty level). Update with new stats at the end of each round.

Let's see you talk your way out of this

A game for one or more players, using a single six-sided die and a way to keep track of your score.

The mechanic is thus: you begin with a score of -10 and must roll until you have achieved a positive score, 0 or -30. Rolls of 2, 3 and 4 are added to your score. Rolls of 1, 5 or 6 are subtracted from your score. If you make improvements to your score three times in a row, you are awarded a bonus three points.

What does it all mean? Just this: you have been caught in a compromising situation and must try to charm, lie and ingratiate your way out of it. To do so, however, is to risk further offence and distrust. A score of -30 represents you having exhausted the patience of all concerned and condemned yourself to severe punishment.

If there are two or more players, those not rolling the die may choose to roleplay as the party being prevailed upon, becoming ever more mollified as the player's score goes up or increasingly furious and incredulous as it goes down. The player rolling the die may also choose to offer specific excuses or other confections to accompany their rolls.

EXAMPLE GAME:

THE SCENARIO: You chose to wear the universe as a ball gown. You then trapped its hem in the door-jamb, and in so doing put a rent in it, all the way through, and now you are naked and the universe is in two.

CULPRIT: To be fair, it did look good on me ...

>   *Rolls 4. Score: -6*

OTHERS: This much we concede.

CULPRIT: ... and I had nothing else to wear.

>   *Rolls 5. Score: -11*

OTHERS: Ridiculous. You have a wardrobe full of halters and sheath dresses.

CULPRIT: In any case, they had it coming.

>   *Rolls 5. Score: -16*

OTHERS: Everybody in the universe 'had it coming'? Can you hear yourself right now?

CULPRIT: All I mean is, it was bound to happen eventually.

Rolls 3. Score: -13

OTHERS: That's as may be.

CULPRIT: What I've really done is exposed a weakness in the fabric of the universe.

Rolls 4. Score: -9

OTHERS: Are you saying now that you were performing some sort of altruistic act?

CULPRIT: I'm saying we are all better off for my mishap, embarrassing as it was.

Rolls 2. Bonus +3 for three consecutive successful rolls. Score: -4

OTHERS: It's hard to argue with your point. But still, the universe is in two –

CULPRIT: Also, I look great naked.

Rolls 4.
Score: 0

OTHERS: "… He's not wrong."

FURTHER SCENARIOS TO TRY

Your foe lies outstretched beneath the tree, the half-eaten apple of your wrath beside him.

All about you are feathers and smashed eggs.

You have turned this court room into a bawdy bathhouse.

Sister Josephine, the abbess has discovered you are indeed no nun.

You've returned without gold, without victory and with not a one of the young men and women you summoned so vociferously to your cause.

It was *you* who knocked over the lamp in Thomas Farriner's bakery.

Debris and disease bloom, it seems, wherever you've dragged your shadow.

Inevitably: you have eaten the plums that were in the icebox.

LENNI SANDERS / JAMES VARNEY

That's no ant!

(A game for two or more players)

Nothing lasts forever, and change is good.

The game begins when a player quickly draws a small object, such as a raisin, a pin, or an ant. They must announce 'I've drawn a _____.'

The next player declares, 'That's no _____!' and adds to the drawing, to transform it into something else. They then announce 'It's a _____!' and the game continues. Make a tally to count the turns.

If you are having difficulty identifying a new picture within the existing drawing, it helps to turn it upside down, or let your eyes go out of focus, or remove your glasses, or put on someone else's glasses, or step back, or have a bit of a cry, or ask someone else to describe it to you, or eat a hot chili, or go to another room and try to remember the picture and re-enter, or view it through a very critical eye as if the other player is an artistic rival and you know for certain the hack cannot do anything correctly.

The game ends when either you cannot find a way to transform the picture, or it has become such a work of beauty that you are willing to accept it as it is. When this happens, admit defeat by saying 'Yes - it's a lovely _____!' The last person to add to the drawing in this scenario is the winner of the round.

Title the finished picture *A Lovely* _____ *by* _____. Optional: add the winner's age.

Try experimenting with coloured pens and pencils, or use a stopwatch to give each round a time limit – how many iterations can your drawing go through in five minutes?

Remember: sometimes, it *is* an ant.

GERARD MCKEOWN
Say It Again

When meeting someone with an unusual or distinctive first name, respond like so:

You: [Repeat their name]? Really? Like in the Philip Larkin poem?

Them: Which Philip Larkin poem?

You: *'And of great sadness also.*
  As they wend away
  A voice is heard singing
  Of [their name], *or* [a very similar-sounding name];
  As if the name meant once
  All love, all beauty.'

Say this with utmost seriousness and never admit at any future point to having got the poem wrong.

Bonus points if you successfully repeat the game with a different person in front of the first person without being caught out.

JO BRANDON
Who's Luckiest?

Two or more players pick up a pair of dice each.
> (More reassuring to imagine luck in doubles –
> remember what comes in threes.)

All roll their dice simultaneously.
You can look – or not – at one another's dice.
Then, based only on the numbers you have rolled,
shout: *I'm the luckiest*
> (What is luck? All sixes? Matching pair?
> Consecutive? Total sum?)

if you think you are.
> (NB: After rolling dice with my boyfriend, over and
> over, I have ascertained, scientifically, that I am 16%
> luckier when it comes to rolling snake-eyes.)

If not, stay quiet. Don't tempt fate, keep good fortune stoppered
if you're worried about that sort of thing.

If you're prone to vainglory   or have self-diagnosed
a superiority complex,

I think you'll like this game. I think you'll do really well.

One free maxim per play:

> You make your own luck.

LINDA BLACK

DRAW!

YOU WILL NEED:

a) *Paper [e.g. cold press, hot press, cotton, rough tooth]*
b) *Implements for drawing*
c) *A deck of cards – remove all but the aces & picture cards*

Shuffle → draw a card at random:

Black Jack = !   Red Jack = !!   Black Queen = !!!
Red Queen = !!!!   Black King = !!!!!   Red King = !!!!!!
Black Ace = !!!!!!!   Red Ace = !!!!!!!!

With reference to your card, DRAW as follows:

! a landscape – hills, trees, scarp, sky etc, maybe sea. Add: a starfish, a hanging, a shoe (or boot), tears (or rents) . . . Nothing is wrong.

!! a single central object (torso, skull, heart). Get up, move around. Take a certain length of time. A smallish piece of paper.

!!! that which is large, small and that which is small, large.

!!!! the contours of a reclining figure – hills/valleys/rocks etc. If available, use charcoal (from the burning of wood, peat, bones).

!!!!! starting in the top left-hand corner. Move down in inclinations till the page is almost filled. Hoops, loops, dogs, cats, heads, hats, whatever.

!!!!!! household objects, not as they are but what you see in them. A dishcloth could be the sea.

!!!!!!! cross-eyes ,, two noses ,, two mouths ,, two pairs of ears ,, two necks,, two chests,, multiple feet (your decision) – wheresoever they belong.

!!!!!!!! with the opposite hand: 'An awful flower grew in his brain like a fierce geranium that shattered its pot.'

---

1. from 'Three Players of a Summer Game' by Tennessee Williams

EILEEN RAMOS
Show and Tall Tale
(A game for three or more players)

Start by finding a thrift shop, antique store, flea market, or other shop that sells a wide range of used goods. One player takes the role of judge. The other players are each given five minutes to search for three disparate items and concoct a story involving all of them.

When relaying their story back to the group, it's preferable that players are able to show each item in turn and describe its traits in a way that enhances the story. They should also add an otherworldly element to their tale, whether based in fantasy, sci-fi, horror, or magical realism. It does not have to take place in the present time.

The judge chooses the better story based on: cohesion, originality, and the challenge posed by the items. A narrative about a 1960s voting pin, a kitty gravy boat, and a neon sign of rolling dice should be considered more daring than one about a rubber ducky, a beach towel and a bath bomb.

In subsequent rounds, different players take on the role of judge. If a player is imaginative enough to connect their current story back to one told previously, the judge should take that into account. Between them, players should aim to generate a cycle of interrelated stories over multiple rounds. This can then be expanded into a mythic universe as the game continues to be played on different occasions.

Time travel should be used sparingly, if at all.

LCC / GEN ZENDAHL / JOE RAUDI
The Glass Bead Game

The Glass Bead Game is a game of speaking and listening. It offers a structure for constructive dialogue, creative exploration and collaborative sensemaking.

Gameplay:

Two players take five turns, each lasting one minute. The players choose a topic (the 'bead') about which they wish to speak. Taking turns, they improvise a dialogue.

1. After the bead is chosen, the players decide who will speak first.
2. Both players wait one minute in silence before beginning.
3. Player One speaks for one minute on the bead. Player Two listens.
4. When Player One's minute has finished, Player Two takes their turn. Player Two attempts to build on Player One's contribution while adding their own perspective. Player One listens.
5. The players continue to alternate until each has had five turns.

Three Principles:

– Respect the turn. Players must be silent when it is not their turn to speak.
– Listen closely. Players should not plan what they are going to say while the other player is speaking.
– Avoid ego. Players should try to avoid 'I' and 'you', favouring 'we' instead.

Notes:

1. A timer is needed, preferably one which does not need to be reset each time.
2. Players are encouraged to experiment with the number and length of turns, the number of players and what constitutes a bead. Beads do not have to be abstract concepts; they can be images, songs or recipes, for example.
3. The game can also be played with multiple beads – a bead string. Two beads might be chosen at the start of the game, or additional beads may be introduced at regular or random intervals during play.
4. The game can be played using other expressive tools. Players could choose to improvise music, dance, art or writing, rather than speech, or use different combinations in a single session.

MARY WHITE
A Book House for Paper Dolls
from The Child's Rainy Day Book *(1905)*

Any little girl who is looking for a home for a family of paper dolls will find a book the very best kind of a house for them. And then such fun it will be to furnish it! First comes the house-hunting. A large, new blank book with unruled pages would be best of all, and that is what we want if we can get it, but of course not all doll families can live in such luxury. An old account book with most of its pages unused will make an excellent house. I have even known a family of dolls to be cheerful and happy in an old city directory.

It will be easy to find furniture in the advertising pages of magazines. Rugs can be cut from pictures in the same magazines and bits of wallpaper used for the walls. Tissue paper of different colours and papers with a lace edge make charming window curtains, while thicker fancy papers may be used for *portieres*. On the cover of the book a picture of the doorway may be pasted. The first two pages are of course the hall. For this you will need a broad staircase, hall seat, hardwood floor and rugs, with perhaps an open fireplace or a cushioned window seat to make it look hospitable. Try to find furniture all about the same size. If you cannot, put the smaller pieces at the back of the room and the larger ones toward the front.

Next there will be the drawing room to furnish, then the library, the dining room and pantry, not forgetting the kitchen and laundry. Use two pages for each room, leaving several between the different rooms, so that the book shall not be too full at the front and empty at the back. If it does not close easily remove some of the blank pages. Cut out the different pieces of furniture as carefully as possible, paste them in as neatly as you can, and you will have a book house to be proud of.

Flowered papers will be the best for the bedrooms, or plain wall papers in light colours; and with brass bedsteads, pretty little dressing tables and curtains made of thin white tissue paper (which looks so like white muslin), they will be as dainty as can be. Now and then through the book it is interesting to have a page with just a bay window and a broad window seat with cushions and pillows—as if it were a part of a long hall. Hang curtains of coloured or figured paper in front of it so that they will have to be lifted if anyone wants to peep in. When you have finished the bathroom, playroom, maids' rooms and attic there will still be the piazza, the garden, the stables and the golf course (covering several pages), to arrange. If you have a paint box and can colour tastefully you will be able to make your book house even more attractive than it is already.

TRADITIONAL

Hyakumonogatari Kaidankai

(A Gathering of One Hundred Supernatural Tales)

A parlour game from 17th-century Japan, to be played after nightfall.

Arrange 100 lit candles in a circle in a room, and position a single mirror on the surface of a table. In a separate room, players take turns telling scary stories. At the end of each story, the teller must make their way to the room with the candles and blow a single one out, then glance into the mirror before rejoining the other players. As the night goes on and more tales are told, the room with the candles becomes darker and darker, and the boundary between the spirit world and ours grows thinner. It is a brave player who dares blow out the final candle.

In Japanese culture, there are various games that turn creative expression into a social affair. In the late 19th century, *Ukiyo-e* artist Kawanabe Kyōsai attended raucous, sake-fuelled calligraphy and painting parties called *shogakai* (書画会). Around the same time, *renga* (連歌) sessions became popular, in which poets worked through the night to create collaborative linked verse, a form dating back to the 8th century CE. The game described on the opposite page, *Hyakumonogatari Kaidankai* (百物語怪談), was played by members of the samurai class as early as 1660, and served as a test of their courage as well as their storytelling prowess.

    Games have a tendency to amalgamate different kinds of activity and priority in this way, becoming arenas in which normal social conventions are mixed up or mutated. As such, they frequently bring forth, like lost spirits, facets of our own personalities we aren't used to seeing. Perhaps in playing them, we do not so much act out a role as allow something to be acted *through* us?

LENNI SANDERS / JAMES VARNEY
Kill ... kill ... kill!
(A game for two or more players)

Regretfully, it cannot be helped – we must solemnly decide whose life cannot be spared.

Players take turns to name three people who must die. They can be celebrities, friends (including other players), family, or fictional characters.

The next player carefully chooses three adverbs to describe how they would dispatch each poor soul. Adverbs can be chosen for their emotional weight (for example 'sadly' if you are to off a beloved friend) or for their aptness, their comic value.

For example, Bernard Matthews might be killed 'porkily' (it's up to you together to decide what that means). This game is at its most amusing when the deaths dealt are cartoonish, ridiculous or impossible. Any sincerity is just upsetting for all involved.

Once you have announced your deaths, consider drawing for each a gravestone or monument with the other players. The monument need not be made of stone - perhaps this sombre marker of a life departed is the peel from an orange; or a discarded burger wrapper; or writing in sand on a beach.

This is a good game to play via text message, or on paper in a loud room. You can push receipts across a table in the pub to scribble on – in this version any number of players can swap papers at once – or if separated on a train carriage, take it in turn to text across three names, then the corresponding deaths. Of course, you can play this game aloud as well – if played correctly, however, this game should sound like wicked scheming and may therefore be incriminating. Remember, you are under no obligation to enact these killings and we do not encourage this.

Memento mori!

NOTES AND ACKNOWLEDGMENTS

Seb Manley's monster card artwork dates back to approximately 1989, when he was seven years old.

'Stakeout' contains lines from the following didactic poems: *Ars amatoria* by Ovid (2AD); 'An Essay on Man: Epistle 1' by Alexander Pope (1733); 'Desiderata' by Max Ehrmann (1927); 'Advice to a Girl' by Sara Teasdale (1933).

A comprehensive version of the rules to Jetan is available online, published by L. Lynn Smith et al.

'Knuckle Bones' is reproduced from *The Boy's Own Book of Indoor Games and Recreations* (1890), a selection by various contributors, edited by G. A. Hutchison.

'Hot Cockles' and 'I apprenticed my son' are reproduced from *Cassell's Book of In-Door Amusements, Card Games and Fireside Fun* (3rd ed., 1881) by various authors.

'Queen Anne and her Maids' has been altered from the original, which did not imply any attempt on her life.

'Conundra' is based on 'Hiding the Thimble', from *Kate Greenaway's Book of Games*.

'The Glass Bead Game' was inspired by the 1943 Hermann Hesse novel *Das Glasperlenspiel*. LCC, Gen Zendahl and Joe

Raudi created their game after studying previous iterations of Hesse's fictional game created by others. They blended their prototype with modern game design theory and a chess clock timer to reach the final version.

All unattributed pieces come either from anonymous sources, or are the work of the editors.

CONTRIBUTORS

LINDA BLACK is a UK poet and artist. She is the editor of *Long Poem Magazine* and has published five collections, the latest being *Then* (Shearsman Books 2021).
⊕ lindablack.co.uk ⊕ longpoemmagazine.org.uk

JO BRANDON was born in 1986 and is based in West Yorkshire. Jo has a pamphlet, *Phobia*, and two full-length collections, *The Learned Goose* (2015) and *Cures* (2021), both with Valley Press. Jo is a poet, librettist, freelance poetry editor and was Bradford Literature Festival's first Digital Poet in Residence.
⊕ jobrandon.com 🐦 jobrandonpoet

SUSAN COOLIDGE (1835-1905) was an Ohio-born children's author who served as a nurse in the American Civil War. She is best remembered for her *What Katy Did* books, featuring the scrappy, daydreaming Katy Carr.

CHARLES COTTON (1630-1687) was a poet and writer from Staffordshire. His most prominent works include translations of Michel de Montaigne, contributions to *The Compleat Angler* and the compilation of leisure compendium *The Compleat Gamester*.

EDWIN EVANS-THIRLWELL (he/him) writes videogame criticism for places like *Edge* and *Wired*, and verse for places like *Osmosis* and *Burning House Press*. His projects include decks of poetry cards that describe solar systems and gardens. He is very interested in analog, process-based poetry, erasure literature and texts that are in some way executable, like code, spells or recipes.

🐦 dirigiblebill

GILES GOODLAND co-wrote *Surveyor's Riddles* (Sidekick Books, 2015) with Alastair Noon. His most recent book is *Civil Twilight* (Parlor Press, 2022).

KATE GREENAWAY (1846-1901) was an English artist, writer and children's book illustrator. She became well-known for a style of painted illustration that depicted children in Regency-era dress.

CLIFF HAMMETT is a creative tinkerer, critical maker and computational meddler. His experiments work between digital, technical and environmental cultures, to cross-pollinate techniques and open up difficult issues to varied participants and publics in lively and engaging ways.

We know very little of CAPTAIN A. S. HARRISON.

CHARLOTTE HEATHER's writing explores bodies experiencing chronic illness and disability, often intersecting with gender and sex. They are a member of Resting Up Collective and founder of *the remote body*. Their work has appeared in *Hotel*, *Spam Zine* and *Lighthouse Journal*. Charlotte is currently editing a pamphlet concerning RPGs

and illness while teaching creative writing.
🐦 Lottyyy 📷 Lottyyyy

SEB MANLEY makes small games and toys.
📷 FalseForestToys

In 2017 GERARD MCKEOWN was shortlisted for The Bridport Prize, and in 2018 he was longlisted for The Irish Book Awards' Short Story of the Year. His work has been featured in a number of journals and anthologies and broadcast on BBC Radio 4.
🌐 gerardmckeown.co.uk 🐦 gerardmckeown

ASTRA PAPACHRISTODOULOU is a PhD researcher and tutor at the University of Surrey focusing on sculptural poetics in the Anthropocene. She is the author and editor of several books and anthologies of poetry, and her work has appeared in UK and international magazines including *Ambit*, *Berkeley Poetry Review* and *Bee Craft*. Astra is the founder of Poem Atlas, an exhibition platform and publisher of visual poetry, and her work has been exhibited in a range of venues including the Poetry Café and Kew Gardens.
📷 heyastranaut 🐦 heyastranaut

CAMILLE RALPHS has two published pamphlets, *Malkin: An ellegy in 14 spels* (The Emma Press, 2015) and *uplifts & chains* (If A Leaf Falls Press, 2020), with another pamphlet forthcoming in 2023. She writes the 'Averse Miscellany' column for *Poetry London*, conducts the 'Poem's Apprentice'

interview series for *Poetry Birmingham Literary Journal* and is Poetry Editor at the *TLS*.
🐦 CamilleRalphs_

EILEEN RAMOS is a bipolar Filipina-American writer, mental health advocate, editor, and performer. She enjoys playing and experimenting with narrative while engaging the world outside the screen. A book hoarder and cigar box collector, she adores creating gifts for strangers and loved ones.
🌐 eileenramos.com 🐦 wordsiheld 📷 wordsiheld

JOE RAUDI, GEN ZENDAHL and LCC were part of the Arch collective which developed the Glass Bead Game during the COVID 19 pandemic. They are based in England, Wales and Belgium, respectively.

CONWENNA RAY is chiefly an anthropologist and lepidopterist, whose most notable work is *The Earshot Songbook*. Her mystery novels include *Micro Machines* and *Observe, If You Will*.

SQUAMATE & RUNG live by the River Wear in County Durham. They have both worked as structural engineers and games testers, and volunteer at Lambton Exotic Rescue.

Writers JAMES VARNEY and LENNI SANDERS have previously collaborated on the poetry EP *bout bloody time* (2015). James is a theatremaker whose recent work includes *Prince Gorge*, a narrative poem performed with a live band. Lenni's debut pamphlet *Poacher* came out with the Emma Press in 2019.

Scunthorpe-born ROB WALTON lives in Whitley Bay. His poetry has been published by Macmillan, The Emma Press, *Culture Matters*, *The Morning Star*, *Strix*, *The Interpreter's House*, *Butcher's Dog*, *Atrium* and others. Rob collated the New Hartley Memorial Pathway text. His debut collection *This Poem Here* was published by Arachne Press in 2021.
🐦 robwaltonwriter

H. G. WELLS (1866-1946) was a prolific writer across many genres, and one of the earliest science-fiction authors. His contemporary Joseph Conrad declared of him, "O Realist of the Fantastic!" Wells' best-known works include *The Time Machine*, *The Island of Doctor Moreau*, *The Invisible Man* and *The War of the Worlds*.

MARY WHITE (1869-1952) wrote several books for young readers, including *The Child's Rainy Day Book*, *The Book of Games*, *How To Make Pottery* and *The Book of Children's Parties*.

THANK YOU FOR YOUR ATTENTION

THE HIPFLASK SERIES

is an improvised dance of unusual forms and genres, played out across four collaborative, pocket-sized collections. Each book comprises a selection of works that skirt close to (or cross the border into) poetic composition, revealing the dynamic relationship between poetry and other kinds of writing. The major theme of each is extrapolated from one or other of these key aspects of modern poetry – play, appropriation, subtext *and* conflict *– but the result is a series that occupies its own strange niche: mutant miscellanies, oddball assortments. Good for a nip or a slug or a long, deep swig.*

SIDEKICK BOOKS

is a London-based small press specialising in collaborative works and experiments in genre.